# Strength of Heart

*A story of Family, Faith, and Fortitude*

## 5 Principles to Owning Your Life

Cim Carver

For Joshua and Elizabeth
—never forget the miracles that you are.

# CONTENTS

# ACKNOWLEDGMENTS

To my wife Katie.  My everything for time and all eternity.
To my parents who instilled in me a love of family.
To my good friend E.H. who pushed me to finish this.

The bucket list has one less box to check.

# PROLOGUE

My legs flinched involuntarily with every bump in the road as the cracked vinyl of the seats in the old school bus pinched the back of my bare legs. I tried to shift their position to avoid the cracks, but every inch of the seat had one.

Nothing about this moment felt comfortable.

Sitting there, I looked out the window at the road, illuminated by the yellow lights on the side of the bus, and watched the painted lane dividers on the road go by. The cold of the early Idaho morning caused the window to fog slightly as my breath met the glass. Beyond the glow of the yellow lights, the world around me was flat and black. As I sat there in the dark, my mind successfully muted the conversations going on around me, and for that, I was grateful. Honestly, I was glad it was dark because I've never been good at hiding my emotions.

And that morning, I had a lot of emotions running through me. I was beyond nervous, I was scared, and I was way out of my element. From the moment I arrived to wait for the bus, I knew that I had bitten off more than I could chew. But, I had to do this. There was no other choice and no going back now.

"What have I got myself into?" I quietly mumbled.

I reluctantly pulled my eyes away from the window and back to the people sitting around me. I felt like I stood out like a sore thumb. Not only was this my first race of any kind, I was doing a freaking marathon. What kind of an idiot decides to do a marathon without ever having done a 5k, a 10k…or any 'k' whatsoever?

Well, I guess I had the answer to that question—that kind of idiot was me.

In my mind, nearly every one of the other runners looked like Olympic gold medalists compared to me. I couldn't help but compare their runner's shoes and gear to my old beat-up cross-trainers, cut-off t-shirt, old basketball shorts (that also doubled as pajamas, by the way), and my golf visor. It was the best gear I had, but it was obviously lacking. I felt like we couldn't be more different, and that I couldn't be any less prepared.

And then, I noticed a handful of older, somewhat heavy-set runners wearing knee braces and headbands. They clearly weren't there to be competitive, and so I found some comfort in their presence, thinking, "if they can do this, I can do this."

My self-consciousness wasn't helped by the smallness of the crowd. There was no blending in for me at this inaugural marathon—I was on one of just two old school buses carrying fewer than one hundred runners to the starting line.

But, I reminded myself that I wasn't there to blend in, for personal glory, for the challenge, or for any other reason I could imagine.

I was there for my family.

I was there, because out of the rubble of an impossible situation, I was trying to clear a path forward for us.

A flood of emotions welled up inside of me as images and thoughts of the past year filled my mind. I quickly returned my gaze to the safety of the window. Then, out of the security of the early morning darkness, the driver's voice came over the bus' intercom...

"The drive we're making to the starting line follows much of the course you'll be running today. I wish all of you crazy people the best of luck!" While the comment elicited some laughter from the other runners, it absolutely scared me. Attempting to fight back the crushing anxiety I was feeling, I focused on the painted yellow lines on the road as we sped by.

There was no way that I had run anywhere near this distance during my two months of pseudo-training. No way. As the waves of trepidation continued to crash against me, I knew one thing for sure: there really was no other option for me, or for us.

I knew had to do this, no matter what. Too much was riding on it for me to turn back now.

# INTRODUCTION

*"It is not the critic who counts; not the man who points out how the strong man stumbles, or where the doer of deeds could have done them better. The credit belongs to the man who is actually in the arena, whose face is marred by dust and sweat and blood...who spends himself in a worthy cause; who at the best knows in the end the triumph of high achievement, and who at the worst, if he fails, at least he fails while daring greatly, so that his place shall never be with those cold and timid souls who neither know victory or defeat."*

*– Theodore Roosevelt*

Writing this book has been a labor of love. I've stopped and started a hundred times. I've written, deleted, re-written, and deleted again; section after section trying to get it right. Trying to make sure I convey as clearly as I can, some key concepts and ideas that have helped me and many others to live a happier, more fulfilling life. In order to do this, I mean actually do it, I needed to quiet the fear of sharing this very personal experience in such a public way. Finally, the urging of good friends convinced me to just buckle down and get these words down on paper. The goals that finally pushed me across the finish line were: to give my children the gift of this story (it is their story, after all), to help others who may benefit from the lessons I have learned through this experience, and to give my parents the ability to tell people that their son wrote a book.

You're welcome mom.

In many ways, I feel unqualified for this process, and I'm sure glad that perfection is not a prerequisite for writing. Like many of you, I've struggled throughout my life to stand true to my own voice against relentless self-doubt. But, as I've had the opportunity to mentor and work with many people over the years, I've found that the lessons I learned that day on a lonely road in Idaho, have proven helpful to others almost as much as they have to me. And, I feel that sharing this book pays homage to the experience that shaped my life in such a significant way.

Simply put, this book is about taking ownership of your life. There are **three recurring themes** that I hope you'll pick up on:

1. Life is meant to be lived, and to do that, you've got to be right there, in the arena—not hanging out in the stands.
2. How successful you are in life is directly determined by your ability to embrace, develop, and use the gifts that God gave you.
3. Align your mindset with the type of person you want to become, and refuse to accept a life of mediocrity and passivity.

Look, I know life gets hard sometimes. I also know that

things can go downhill in an instant. On the occasions when you feel like you've been hit by a ton of bricks, it can seem easier to just throw your hands in the air and say it's too much.

It also seems easier to place blame on anything and anyone, and to think that the best course of action is to just do nothing and to play it safe. However, I have learned that this response does not propel people forward; in fact, it holds them back, lessens the joys of life, and cheats them of incredible experiences.

Instead, when you are in control of your life and are able to leverage your choices and actions to push you in the direction you want to go—regardless of what's happening around you.

The day you decide to consciously own your life, you become free—free from feeling controlled, free from the paralyzing fear of the unknown, free to chart your own course, free to feel peace and happiness, and free to hope and dream to your heart's content.

When you own your life, you go from challenge to challenge with a smile on your face; not because you enjoy tough times, but because you know you can do hard things and reap the benefits that come from pushing through them.

Sounds good, right?

That's because it is. It's a fundamental principle that supports success in anything worth accomplishing. But, living this way isn't easy for a lot of people. It requires persistent work and conscious discipline. It is a great prize that is won through purposeful, consistent effort—which is why most people don't do it.

Why is that? Why would someone deny themselves such a valuable prize?

Unfortunately, my experience has been that most people have been unintentionally taught and conditioned to think 'dependently.' Whether they have previously been rewarded for people-pleasing behavior, or, they have been taught to believe that dreaming big, taking risks, and standing out is irresponsible, most people are relentlessly coached throughout their lives to play small. Many life experiences and influences shape the belief that there is security in embracing mediocrity, and in feeling a sense of safety and assuredness in the crowd.

And the crowd does feel safe; it feels comfortable. But it only feels that way because it never requires you to grow. Instead, it encourages you to give up ownership of your life and just let it happen to you—instead of you happening to life.

If this sounds like you, it's time for you to wake up! Stop pretending to be unaware that you're not living up to your divinely-ordained potential. Acknowledge the fact that you can be more, and that you want to be more. No more of this, 'sheep mindlessly following a herd,' routine, ok?

Life's journey isn't about waiting for someone else to tell you what to do, it's about you asking yourself: "What do I want to do? Who do I want to become?" and, "How can I be the best I can be?" Then, it's about aligning your choices and actions accordingly—especially when so many obstacles and strong headwinds are trying to push you in a different direction.

Ultimately, that is what this book is about: how to take ownership of your life as you work your way through it. I'll share my personal journey of self-discovery, and explain what I learned along the way.

As cliché as it sounds, my most sincere wish is that you will come away from reading this book with greater clarity, and with the courage to do whatever it takes to live on your own terms. I'm grateful that this book found its way to you. I hope that it will help you in some way.

This is a true story.

# CHAPTER 1

**Principle 1**: Learn to Live Purposefully

*"Our focus is our reality. What we choose to focus on becomes our world. It produces our thoughts, values, attitudes, and beliefs."*

*– David J. Lieberman*

O ver the years, I've learned that people only do things consistently if they matter to them. I've learned that you can give the same opportunity to two people in similar life situations, but the person who identifies with why that opportunity is important to them, and then uses that purpose to drive their actions, will be the person who reaps the reward.

Why?

Because anything worthwhile in your life is always earned, it's not just given to you. These things require discipline and sacrifice and that won't happen unless there is a valuable, understandable purpose behind them.

Now, most people understand this concept logically, but emotionally, they secretly hope that they'll just win the lottery and get everything they ever wanted without having to pay the price required to earn it. People waste years of their life secretly harboring this mindset—going through the motions, paying lip-service to the things they say they want to do, but never really committing themselves to them.

Owning your life starts by learning to live more purposefully. Meaning, you know what you want, and you know why you want it. You align your actions to achieve it, and you hold yourself accountable for the choices you make along the way.

Starting to live your life more purposefully isn't easy—there is a 'cost' associated with it. This can be a cost in time, effort, convenience, comfort, or money. You need to embrace the sometimes inconvenient fact that these costs are part of the process and not waste time complaining about them.

Often, I see that some people struggle to understand what true commitment really looks like. Most people give up too early in their journey to effect change, because their commitment is being tested for the first time, and that is hard. These individuals have good intentions, but they lack the true commitment to stay the course.

You see, most people aren't used to living a life of intention. They may not have a vision for what they want their life to look like, or for the kind of person they want to be.

Their lack of purpose means that they are allowing others to shape their life, and they perhaps feel trapped and unable to change course.

But, the good news is that change is possible.

✻ ⌐The sum of all of your choices going forward —starting right now—will create your reality for tomorrow. ⌐

Over the years, I've seen people in the poorest of circumstances; with no 'connections' or 'inside access' do incredible things simply by taking responsibility for their choices. They own every aspect of their life; the ups and downs, the highs and lows. They understand that success in life is a package deal, as opposed to an à la carte experience where they pursue the path of least resistance.

Conversely, I've also seen people born with incredible connections and advantages live a largely irrelevant life because they refused to take responsibility for their choices. They act as though they are entitled to have a great life.

Regardless of the hand that life has dealt you, it's choices and actions that ultimately determine the outcome.

Too often, people don't recognize the power of their choices. As a result, they can easily end up giving this power away as they allow their emotions to take over and, inevitably, adopt a victim mindset.

When they disengage from their values and goals, they can become a victim of circumstances, a victim of their current environment, and a victim of the choices of others. The longer they hold onto a victim mindset, the longer they will remain powerless.

However, it is so important to remember that this power can be taken back at any time. No permission needs to be granted—ultimately, the choice is theirs to redefine their goals and to re-establish a healthy and productive mindset.

Since owning your life is about purposefully and consciously aligning your actions and choices with the direction you want to go, it's important to clearly understand who you want to be and what you stand for.

While this may sound like common sense, in my experience, it isn't common practice for many people.

# The Calm Before the Storm

It's estimated that over 108 billion people have lived on the earth.

That's a lot of people.

When I consider that, I recognize that I hit the lottery. I was lucky enough to be born into a country that protects personal freedoms, that values human rights, and that has an economic engine that rewards initiative.

But, more than that, I hit the jackpot when it came to my family. I have two parents who love me unconditionally. From birth onward, and even through those awful teenage years, I have never doubted their love. I've never taken this for granted because I know that not everyone has that experience. I was raised in a home where love of family was always paramount. Did we fight? You'd better believe we did. Did we always agree? Heck no. But, there was always an understanding in our family that we looked out for each other, and that family was the most important thing.

I am the oldest of seven children and the seven of us were born within ten years of each other. For a decade, my mom was changing cloth diapers (as she is always quick to point out) and breastfeeding. My parents sacrificed a lot for us, as parents often do.

My father always worked at least two jobs, often three, to try to provide for us. During an especially tight financial time, I remember getting up with my dad very early in the morning to deliver newspapers. My brother and I would pile into our family station wagon, go pick up the stack of papers, and then sit in the back of the station wagon and work. One of us would roll up the newspaper, while the other one put rubber bands around it and placed it in the front seat for my dad. He would then toss it out his window and onto the subscriber's driveway. This took a few hours, and usually included at least one stop for either my brother or I to throw up from the combination of newspaper fumes and the unrelenting swaying motion that tossed us around in the back of the car.

Good times.

We'd return home, my dad would get ready to go teach, and my brother and I would get ready to go to school. As if that didn't make the day long enough, most of the time, my dad would go right from teaching to another job until late into the evening.

My mom would usually let us stay up each night to wait for dad to come home, and as he'd slowly walk through the door exhausted, he'd kneel down, put his head on the floor and cover it with his arms and play what he called 'family rock.'

We would climb all over him like a jungle gym, jumping off his back, and sliding down his legs while he stayed curled up in a ball on his knees. Every once in a while, his arm would come to life and grab one of us and tickle us for a few moments before returning to protect the back of his head. I'd later find out that 'family rock' was how my exhausted father, weary from the day, would try to spend time with us; to give us his love and attention the best way he could when he could barely keep his eyes open.

They both sacrificed so much for us.

That was just one of countless examples where my parents taught me the importance of family. My parent's actions ingrained in me the unshakable, foundational belief that parents do whatever is needed, no matter the sacrifice, for their family.

Maybe it was because I was the oldest and often had to take on significant responsibilities in the home, but I grew up viewing myself as a parent to my siblings. And, instead of resenting the role (like I know they sometimes resented me for being the bossy older brother), I grew up valuing it. It was part of my identity and how I saw myself. As I got older, I always knew that I would be a father to my own family someday. It was more than just something I hoped would happen—in my mind it was going to happen.

And then it did.

In the fall of 1996, I took a beautiful girl named Katie on a date for the first time. I was just 21 years old and thought she was way out of my league, but for some reason, she agreed to go out with me. To my surprise, she continued to want to hang out with me, and six months later, we were married.

All of my adult life, I've had people tell me that I got married too young. My reply has always been that when you meet Katie, you'll see why. I wasn't going to risk losing her, and if she was willing to marry a schmuck like me, well, I wasn't going to miss out on it just because I was young.

Did I miss out on some partying because I got married so young? Probably.

Did I miss out on some typical college experiences? Without a doubt.

Could I have found someone better than Katie if I'd waited and dated more? Heck no.

Getting married at a young age wasn't a hard decision for me because I wasn't focusing on what I would be missing; I was focused on becoming who I wanted to be. I wanted to be successful in my career—to do something that mattered and that made a difference in the lives of others (just like my father did as a teacher), and I wanted to be a dad.

Over the next few years, Katie and I went through the typical ups and downs associated with newlyweds. We had very little money and we were both going to school. But, by taking it one day at a time, we eventually figured it out. After this customary adjustment period, we felt it was time to start our family. Our first pregnancy ended in miscarriage, which was a very difficult experience for both of us. However, the second pregnancy went full term and, in June of 1999, Katie gave birth to our first child, our son Caleb.

To say that I was a proud father would be an understatement. I was ridiculously proud. Caleb was my boy—my first child! He had these dark brown eyes and a smile that would melt your heart. He was the first grandchild for my parents, and my entire family constantly doted on him.

And, like most first-time parents, I was totally unrealistic in my visions of the future for Caleb…and oblivious to how annoying I was to other people when I'd talk about him.

In my mind, he was going to cure cancer, bring peace to the Middle East, achieve athletic greatness…and then graduate High School. I would incessantly point out how cool he was — quietly comparing him to other kids his age, and completely convinced, in my mind anyway, that he was clearly ahead of the pack.

Seriously, I was over the top.

But, I couldn't help it. I had been waiting for this for so long. Finally, I was a dad and I wasn't going to screw it up. I was determined to be the best father ever. When my son looked at me or held my hand, when he went to sleep on my chest or smiled at me, I committed again and again to be there for him and to live up to the expectations I had of myself to be the best dad I could be. Having Caleb awakened a deep love inside of me that I never knew was there. If you have kids, you probably know what I'm talking about.

I've always said that sacrifice is only a negative thing when it doesn't have a purpose. I started to understand how my parents were able to sacrifice so much for us once I became a parent myself. The sacrifices of going to school full-time, working full-time, and trying to be a good husband and father, didn't bother me. In my mind, dads sacrificed for their families; that's just what they did.

We didn't have a lot, but we had enough.

It was Katie, me, and Caleb. It was Sunday walks and hours

of nerf basketball after work. It was baby's first Christmas, and a Winnie the Pooh Halloween costume. It was quiet naps in a baby swing, first steps, and first words.

It was a time of life I'll always cherish because things felt just like they were supposed to be.

It was the calm before the storm.

*Myself and my parents not long after I was born.*

*Our first family picture not long after Caleb was born.*

# CHAPTER 2

## Principle 2: Be Committed

### Part 1 - Attack Obstacles with Belief, Not Fear

*"When we believe in the obstacle more than in the goal, which will inevitably triumph?"*

*– Ryan Holiday*

As you start to live more purposefully, you can expect to face obstacles and experience some push back. It is just part of the process and, if you've prepared yourself ahead of time, you won't emotionally overreact when it happens.

When facing an unexpected obstacle, people can quickly abandon so much of what they said they were committed to. In an effort to avoid feeling like they're failing and to avoid pain, the tendency is often to retreat to a place of lesser commitment.

The true test of your commitment to a goal or task only occurs when you meet a roadblock. In fact, you'll never know how committed you are until you are challenged. And, if running away is your solution when your commitment is challenged, running away will eventually become a habit anytime obstacles arise in the process of achieving a goal.

And, as discussed earlier, how you react to obstacles is a choice.

While knowing the purpose behind what you do is the first principle to owning your life, aligning your mindset is the second.

At its core, the choice you have when confronting an obstacle is to choose to respond with a mindset of belief, or a mindset of fear. Responding with a belief mindset happens when you're focused on what you're trying to achieve—it's playing to WIN. However, reacting from a mindset of fear is a defensive reaction that focuses on the things you don't want to happen. It's playing NOT TO LOSE.

While both mindsets can feel like they're trying to accomplish the same thing, they aren't.

Making choices from a place of fear makes you weaker—it disconnects your heart from your goal, it erodes your commitment, and it can cause you to lose sight of your purpose. And, when actions lack purpose, they're easily abandoned. A fear-oriented mindset can feel safe; it can feel like you're being appropriately cautious and avoiding risk, but that's a lie. This false sense of security is not, in fact, playing it safe—it is playing it soft. So don't fall for this lie because you are capable of so much more.

Conversely, making choices from a place of belief makes you stronger. It is these emotionally charged and anxiety-filled experiences in life that ultimately develop the strength of your character.

To truly own your life, you have to get in the habit of playing to win. I knew that being a great dad was at the core of who I was before Caleb was born. I knew it would be hard work, but I knew it would be worth it. That said, I didn't fully appreciate what it would mean to be worthy of the title of 'dad' in those early days. I thought I was playing to win...but it's easy to play that way when there's no real opposition. However, as obstacles often do, they challenged my purpose, my commitment, and my mindset.

Things were about to get real.

# The Storm Arrives

I could drive the route home from work with my eyes closed and I needed a mindless drive that day. It had been a hectic day—school in the morning, work that afternoon, and I had a lot on my mind. However, as I turned the corner to head to our small apartment, my mind immediately shifted to Caleb. He was almost two years old and, next to Katie, was the center of my world.

He was such a cute boy with a smile that melted hearts. I couldn't have imagined a better baby boy; honestly, in my mind, he was perfect. He was just learning how to shoot baskets on our little nerf hoop in the living room and I couldn't wait to get home and practice with him.

At that time, Katie was pregnant with our second child, and we had recently found out that she was carrying a girl. We had decided to name her Caitlyn, a combination of both of our mother's names. At that point, my life felt like it was pretty much on track. I was finally getting close to graduating with my undergraduate business degree, I was married to a beautiful woman, I had an amazing son, and a daughter was on the way.

I would later look back on that day and realize that it was the final day of calm before the storm hit us. The tide was about to turn.

I parked my car, grabbed my ridiculously heavy school bag, and headed down the steps towards our apartment. I opened the door, anxiously looking for Caleb so we could start playing some hoops. As I entered, I didn't see Caleb, but Katie was sitting on the couch with her feet pulled up underneath her, and tears were slowly streaming down her face.

Something was wrong.

"My cousin came by today and she said we need to get Caleb checked by a doctor."

"Wait...what? What do you mean? Which cousin? Checked for what?" I asked, completely caught off guard.

Katie explained that it was her cousin, Paula, who had visited that day. We had recently been at a family gathering with Paula and her family, and I remember having noticed that her children had some sort of disability, but I hadn't been sure what. Paula had told Katie that Caleb looked to have some of the same symptoms that her boys had shown at the same age.

I couldn't believe it. Sure, we knew that Caleb was behind in a few areas. He was a little slow to walk and to talk, but we had explained that away easily, citing tons of examples of geniuses who had similar delays. This was my boy, after all. He was perfect, and he was going to do great things in his life; I just knew it.

Katie's face, at that moment, however, expressed something quite different. "Paula told me that we should get him tested for something called Fragile X Syndrome," she said in a whispered tone, burdened with fear.

Now, there are times when you can feel your life pivot right under your feet. You can literally feel the world shift—it turns on a dime and you know that things will never, ever be the same again. And when that happens, the natural reaction is to fight it. It creates a deep fear inside of you that causes every part of you to resist it, to deny it, and to convince yourself it isn't true.

I'll never forget that moment when Katie, through tears, said those words to me: 'Fragile X Syndrome'. My world pivoted. It shifted. I felt it and it scared me.

No. No. Please, dear God, no. This is not my plan—this isn't supposed to happen.

We stood there, hugging each other in that small apartment, feeling unmoored and lost. One moment, one conversation and our lives changed forever. In those initial, all-consuming moments of fear, I started fighting the shift I could feel happening...clinging to the reality I had known just a few minutes earlier.

"I doubt she's right, Katie," I tried to say with confidence. "He's way too young to even know, and I wish she wouldn't have even put that in your mind."

"But, what if she's right? What if he has it?" she asked, terrified.

As if he could tell we were talking about him, Caleb came walking out of the back bedroom, nerf ball in hand and smiling from ear-to-ear; full of innocence and joy. He came to me, ready to shoot some baskets. Katie picked him up, I gave

29

him a kiss, but all I felt inside was fear. I had to do something, read something, learn something — anything.

"I'm going to go to my parent's house and get on the internet," I told her. "I want to see the symptoms of Fragile X; I bet we're worrying about nothing," I said, trying to put enough confidence in my voice for the both of us.

My parents lived about 10 minutes away from us, but that drive felt like an eternity. The internet was not widely available at this time, so their house was my closest access point to the information I so desperately needed. I don't remember anything about that drive, other than my mind trying to reassure itself that everything was going to be ok.

However, another voice from deep inside me was whispering, "Cim, be ready."

That voice had first surfaced several months earlier when someone asked if I was concerned that he wasn't yet walking on his first birthday. It was that quiet, yet present, voice that I had tried to avoid for nearly a year — coming up with well-rehearsed rationalizations to explain his delays instead. It had become a quiet game of emotional whack-a-mole in my mind; where these thoughts would rise up in my consciousness and I would beat them back down, but, no matter how hard I tried, I could never shake them completely.

I realized that my heart was already mourning the loss of my life of just a half hour ago, but my mind was still fighting to hang onto the hope that Paula was wrong, and that everything was going to be ok.

I arrived at my parent's house, ran inside and down to their computer without saying a word to my mom. I typed, 'Fragile X Syndrome symptoms in children," into a search engine and watched as the screen filled with results. I clicked on the top link and waited impatiently for the page to load. Then, I started quickly skimming the page and saw a bulleted list of symptoms. I held my breath as I started to read them. With each line that I read, my body went progressively numb, the hair on my neck began to stand up, and my ears started to ring.

With each bullet point, my world got heavier and heavier...darker and darker.

My grand plan, my hopes and dreams, were being destroyed one line at a time on that computer monitor. It was as if someone had spent a week watching Caleb and now was describing him in bullet points. So many of his cute quirks and endearing mannerisms that we loved were laid out before me as characteristics of Fragile X Syndrome.

I couldn't deny it; the whisper in my heart now found an undeniable voice—one that I couldn't beat back any longer. I kept reading, but by now, my entire body was tingling and my legs were shaking. An unrecognizable fear was relentlessly thrashing inside me. As much as I tried, I couldn't tear my eyes away from the screen as I checked one site after another, silently begging to be proven wrong.

My mom, hearing me crying, came into the room and asked to know what was wrong.

"Caleb...he's sick. He's sick, mom. He's not ok," I

stammered.

My mom leaned over the back of the chair, wrapping her arms around me. All I could do was point to the computer screen. Then, I put my head down, body shaking, and wept.

I don't remember much about the rest of that day. I know I tried to pull myself together at my parent's house, and my mom tried to rationalize with me that we still didn't know anything for sure. I managed to convince my brain that there was still a chance we were wrong; but, in my heart, I knew. The little voice that had been trying to prepare me over the past year, the one I kept pushing to the back of my mind because it shook my soul, was right. Caleb wasn't ok. I went home and tried to put on a brave face, but I was so scared.

"We need to get him tested right away," I told Katie. "He has a lot of the symptoms."

Watching my amazing wife, my beautiful companion, my best friend, and the strongest woman I'd ever met, be crushed by this news made me feel even more helpless. We prayed together like we'd never prayed before. "Please, let him be ok Father. We have always tried our best to do what was right. To be good people. Please, if it be thy will, let our son be whole."

I had never felt so helpless in my life.

We had to wait a few weeks before we could get an appointment at the University of Utah to have the test done. In the meantime, we tried to keep our spirits up, clinging to the hope that everything would be ok. But, in our hearts, we already knew.

When we finally got in to see the geneticist, he talked to us about Fragile X, explaining to us that because it was genetic, there was a 50/50 chance that every one of our kids would have the syndrome. He didn't say the words, but I knew he was talking about Caitlyn and the implication that we could be dealing with this all over again in a mere matter of months was terrifying.

The weeks waiting for the test results were full of prayers — we pleaded with God to spare our child and our family from this, but we also asked that we be prepared for whatever His will was.

The day the official diagnosis came we cried, and we realized that the glimmer of hope we'd clung to was officially gone. Caleb had Fragile X Syndrome. Running through my head on a non-stop repeat were the words, "my plan, this wasn't my plan. This isn't right; this isn't how it is supposed to be."

I was unmoored and adrift—both emotionally and spiritually. No one is ever fully prepared to receive news like that, and it hit both of us like a rogue tsunami wave. It felt like the direction of my life had totally shifted. Rationally, I knew that we'd have to figure out a way to go on, but I had no idea how that was going to happen. And, of greater concern, I wasn't sure I even wanted to go on because it meant letting go of a life I thought I was supposed to have, and replacing it with one I didn't want.

# CHAPTER 3

### Principle 2: Be Committed

*Part 2* - *Don't Try and Walk Alone*

*"We are not placed on this earth to walk alone."*

*- Thomas S. Monson*

Being committed to something doesn't mean you have to try and do it alone. It can be hard, at times, to reach out for help. However, pretending that you're not deserving of support, or feeling embarrassed to ask for it, is a very common form of self-sabotage for many people.

When facing inevitable challenges on the road to success, it's important to remember that there is always room on your journey for another person. There is nothing noble about suffering in solitude. Conversely, it is incredibly noble, and even wise, to lock arms with others who can offer support—especially on those tough days when you're barely able to crawl.

During those dark days, life will feel hopeless, it will feel pointless, and it will challenge every bit of you to not withdraw from others.

You may feel ashamed at the intensity of your emotions, and therefore, wish to hide them. Just remember that you are never more relatable to another person than when you're struggling. Learning to lean on others isn't a weakness and it sure doesn't cheapen your eventual victory. In fact, I'd argue that this ability is a sign of strength—to admit our  vulnerability to another human takes a heck of a lot of courage.

I am a spiritual person and I pray. Now, while not every prayer is answered in a way I like, I have never uttered a single prayer that wasn't returned with the peace of knowing that I wasn't alone.

And you are not alone either.

None of us were created to walk through the ups and downs of life alone. In fact, I believe that one of the reasons we experience obstacles is because they tend to humble us, and they redirect our gaze heavenward. It is in these moments  that we remember that our lives have purpose and meaning, and that our Maker has created this journey just for us.

# Seeing the Sunshine and not the Shadow

I would love to be able to say that I was strong during those first weeks after we received Caleb's diagnosis. I wish I could claim that I had what my dad called a 'stiff upper-lip,' and that I bravely navigated those uncertain waters while providing comfort and support for those around me.

Unfortunately, that would be a lie. I was a wreck. My new reality was taking some time to accept and to get used to. I had always been a spiritual person, but after the diagnosis, I felt betrayed, I felt angry, and, for the first time in my life, I felt entitled to blessings that I wasn't receiving. I felt that I deserved better than what I was getting. I realize today that I was using that anger to mask the pain I was experiencing.

If I can make an analogy of my life at that time, it would be that I was merely treading water—trying to keep myself and my family from drowning.

Often, Katie would try and talk with me about things. I could see how she was trying to heal us so we could move forward. But, I didn't want to heal because healing meant accepting things; it meant a recognition that my life had permanently changed. So I brushed off her attempts and continued to try not to feel anything.

Looking back, I realize that I was mourning the death of my son. Not my actual son, of course, but the son whom I had imagined in my mind since my youth; the son who would be a great scholar and athlete, the son who would be a leader among men, and the son who would do incredible things and have limitless potential.

Shortly after his diagnosis, we started seeking out specialists and early intervention programs for Caleb. Now, I loved these people and I knew that these programs were designed to help my son, but I hated them at the same time. I hated them because they served as a constant reminder of this new and heartbreaking reality. I hated them because they made me feel like Caleb was broken, defective, and incomplete. Now, let me be clear—no one treated him this way—I was just stuck in a negative place of bitterness, resentment, and anger.

Whenever I could, I found excuses not to go to the appointments and, looking back on it, it still embarrasses me. Too often, I left my amazing wife to face those challenges alone. And, truthfully, even when I was there in body, my heart remained dark.

I'd be out somewhere and see other children, seemingly perfect and healthy children, running and talking and interacting with their parents, and I'd feel ashamed at the raging jealousy I couldn't help but feel inside. That was supposed to be my life. And, even though I knew it wasn't right, I often found myself comparing my son to those children. I also found myself pushing well-intentioned friends and family members away during this time; I was building protective walls around myself and my little family, and it wasn't healthy.

And then, in the middle of all of this turmoil and grief, our beautiful daughter, Caitlyn, was born.

Caitlyn's birth was anything but traditional as her breech

position forced an emergency caesarean section. Everything and everyone was rushing around Katie, and I felt helpless and overwhelmed. I crouched beside her in the operating room and attempted to bring my brave wife comfort. In fact, when the surgeons began to cut, the epidural hadn't even fully taken effect. Katie could feel a strong burning sensation, but when I suggested we tell the delivery team to wait a few minutes, Katie squeezed my arm and said, "No, just get Caitlyn out. I'll be ok."

My wife is superwoman.

The medicine kicked in a few moments after that initial cut and Caitlyn was born. What followed were bittersweet moments. We were undeniably thrilled to meet our beautiful daughter, and were so happy that she was here to officially join our family. However, we also knew that we needed to get Caitlyn tested for Fragile X, and, as we'd learned since Caleb's diagnosis, early intervention was important.

So, we ordered the test. I remember taking our little baby girl to the doctor, having them prick her heel, and the crying that ensued as they drew blood to send off to be tested. I can still see her blood in that small vile; the blood that gave her life, the blood that could contain 'defective' genetics, and the blood that meant so many things. So, I took what hope I had left in me, and I prayed.

"Please, Father, let her be whole. Let her be spared," was my simple prayer. It was all I could muster to give at that point. A few weeks later, the doctor called with the results.

Caitlyn also had Fragile X.

Both of my babies had this syndrome. Strangely, I expected to feel even more devastated than I already did, but I think that I was pretty numb by this point—and that scared me. While I recognized that the numbness I was experiencing was a fairly normal defense mechanism intended to spare me further pain, it was also preventing me from living.

I did my very best to console my wife and to tell her that we aren't ever given more than we can handle in life, and that we would get through it, but the words felt devastatingly empty to me. As I held my baby girl closer that night, I willed the tears to come. I willed myself to feel—anything at all. It was during this very dark night (literally and emotionally) that I finally started to recognize that I wasn't living up to the type of man my parents raised me to be.

But even with that recognition, I didn't yet know what to do about it. I began to see that, through my selfishness, I was acting like a victim. I was running away from my emotions, abdicating my choices, and letting life happen to me, as opposed to the other way around. And I while I knew better, I wasn't sure how to change.

This recognition weighed on my heart and mind for weeks.

And then, one Thursday afternoon, after yet another specialist's appointment where we listened to more doctors tell us to manage our expectations about Caitlyn, something within me finally started to change.

I remember sitting at my desk, replaying the specialist's words in my mind over and over again, and wallowing in the same self-pity that had become my habitual response at this point. When slowly, an uncontrollable chill began to build in my spine.

Unconsciously, my mind went blank and my eyes closed. And, then, a voice deep within me lovingly spoke, not with audible words, but in a way that gave understanding to my very soul.

It said, "Cim, there will be people who will doubt these precious kids their entire lives, and people who will seek to put limits on them. You can't be one of them. You are their dad. Now, act like it!"

And, just like that, I began to feel a shift.

The weight and darkness I had grown so accustomed to carrying around with me was lifting. I was finally able to see things for what they were, and it allowed me, for the first time since that fateful day when I came home and found Katie crying on the couch, to embrace my new life with my whole heart.

In that instant, I decided to not just accept our new reality, but to love it. I made the decision that day, to focus on the sunshine instead of on the shadow. And then, a simple phrase from the deepest part of my soul escaped as a quiet whisper from my mouth:

"I'm their dad." And then a little louder, "I'm their dad!"

A feeling of warmth came over me; a feeling of love—of being able to give it and to receive it. And then, at long last, a feeling of peace.

I realized that, although my plan had changed and things now looked different than I had initially pictured them, I had beautiful, amazing children who were counting on me to be the best dad I could be. I am not proud of how I reacted during those long, dark, initial months, but I now see that I was doing my best to figure things out. Even in that very troubled time, I never lost my desire to be a good father, and that desire ultimately pushed me forward, and pushed me past those feelings of despair and into a more honest, brave, and capable place.

I was so grateful to have finally reached the point where I had learned what I needed to learn, to have gained the understanding I needed, as well as the perspective I lacked. And, with a tender mercy from God, I was given a shock with an emotional defibrillator that got my heart to fully function again.

Words seem so inadequate to describe the sheer power of that moment. I've written and rewritten this section multiple times, and yet, it always falls short. Spiritual things are learned and understood in spiritual ways, so it should be no surprise that words are insufficient.

But while words aren't enough to relate what that experience was like, the fruits of that experience were undeniable. From that day forward, I started to engage more fully; I cherished every moment I spent with my children, I celebrated their daily progress, and I felt my sense of profound purpose return. Along with my renewed sense of purpose came gratitude, acceptance, and peace.

And, as time tends to do without us realizing it, the days stretched into weeks and the weeks into months. And slowly, this new and unexpected reality evolved into our new normal. It was around the time of Caitlyn's second birthday, that Katie and I found ourselves hesitantly discussing the idea of having more children. It was a scary subject, but both of us wondered if our family was complete.

We had so many questions and so many things to discuss. What if we had another baby and it also had Fragile X—could we raise three kids with special needs? Was it irresponsible of us to bring more kids into our home without understanding the longer-term needs of Caleb and Caitlyn? Were we ready to go through the intense emotional roller coaster again?

Every discussion seemed like it brought up more questions. So, we prayed for guidance and help. We prayed for months to know if our family was complete, and slowly, the answer was given. Undeniably, a strong understanding was laid upon our hearts.

Our family wasn't complete; we weren't finished having children yet.

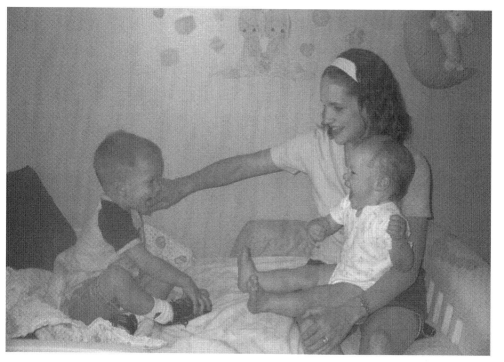

*Katie and the kids. I love this picture because it captures the feeling in our home at this time. I was so glad to finally get to a point where I could see it.*

# CHAPTER 4

## Principle 3: Control the Controllable

*"In life we have two categories of events: those which we can control, and those which we can't control. Success, they say, involves distinguishing between the two and directing your energies toward the controllable, while having the discipline to not waste time and energy on that beyond your control."*

*– Ron Sirak*

There will always be situations and events beyond our control. They push back against your commitments and can even cause you to second guess your efforts to own your life. If you let it, they can take over a large portion of your thoughts and focus, eroding the vital strength you need to keep going in the face of adversity. This is a waste of time and energy!

Look at it this way. When time and energy are given to the things you can't control, you are essentially making yourself less effective when navigating the things that are within your control. If you think about it, there are two parts to the energy you need to own your life—the physical energy to perform the task, and the emotional energy (the 'will') to get it done.

I once read that 70% of the energy required to reach a goal is emotional. If this is true, and my experience to date would concur with this analysis, then your commitment to your goals is powered by your emotional energy more than anything else. And that is powerful stuff.

It would seem, then, that managing this emotional energy is a crucial part of the ability to live your life purposefully. And, I'm sure this comes as no surprise—it all goes back to the idea of choice. Where do you choose to allocate your emotional energy? Is it on things that are within your control? Or, are you mired in a pit of denial, blame, or self-pity like I was during that period of darkness?

In order to develop the mindset and discipline to 'control the controllable,' you will need to do two things:

First, look at your goal and the commitment you've made to it, and then identify the actions you'll need to take to achieve it. Don't overwhelm yourself with a long list of actions. Instead, select 2-3 that you think will have the greatest impact and focus on those.

Second, make a conscious effort to do those 2-3 things BEFORE you do anything else that's goal related. This disciplined approach will help you reach your goals more quickly and with greater success. ⌉

However, I would be remiss if I didn't mention that, while the strategy listed above sounds both logical and doable, there is one problem: solving life's problems isn't always logical. In fact, much of the time it is emotional. And when your commitments are being tried and you are at the end of your rope, it is very easy to abandon your well-practiced discipline of working on the things you can control, and indulge in trying to control the uncontrollable, all over again.

When the going gets tough, many people quickly revert to their old, established habits. They blame. They complain. They rationalize. They justify. They adopt a victim's mindset.

I learned this the hard way when we found out that Caleb, and then Caitlyn, had Fragile X Syndrome. I had to learn to accept the things I couldn't change, to stop wasting energy trying to control things that I couldn't, and to give my focus and emotional energy to the things I could.

Was it easy? No.

Was it worth it? Absolutely yes.

# Moving Forward

The hardest thing about taking a 'leap of faith' is the leaping part.

Philosophically, this is an easy concept to talk about in noble and inspirational terms, but let me tell you, the actual leaping can be anything but noble or inspirational. The process is a relentless, fear-filled battle, where sometimes, the best you can do is just not quit.

In the movie, Indiana Jones and the Last Crusade, Jones has to pass through a series of 'tests' on his way to retrieving the Holy Grail to save his dying father. He has a map and an adventurer's skill-set that get him past flying saw blades and other life-or-death tests. But, the final test is the 'leap of faith' where he faces a long, bottomless, chasm with no visible way to cross. This is a test of his faith; a literal 'leap of faith.'

All the knowledge, training, and skill he possesses as an adventurer and archeologist is useless in that moment, because it isn't that kind of a test. It's a test where he has to take a step into the unknown and have faith that something will be there to keep him from plummeting to his death.

Indiana is unsure of himself, he's scared, he's uncomfortable—but then he remembers his father who needs him, who has always encouraged him to believe, even when there isn't any evidence he should. So, he sticks his foot out over the edge of that bottomless cliff and...takes a step. As his foot comes down, it lands on an invisible bridge. With more confidence, he takes the next step and, soon, the entire bridge becomes visible to him and he is able to run across it.

The powerful message contained in the visual of this story has always stuck with me. And, its poignancy was even more apparent during the period of time where Katie and I were figuring out how to bring these additional children into our family as we felt called to do. We, too, had to step forward, with no idea how, or even if, our feet would land on solid ground.

We had people tell us we were crazy, and that it was irresponsible for us to have more children when the ones we had would clearly need more of our time than 'normal' kids. Katie and I had already discussed all of these issues. We also had people on the other side, encouraging us, and not understanding why this was such a tough decision.

At this point, we knew one thing—our family was not yet complete, so we had to figure this out.

We looked into adoption, but were told that because we already had two children, our chances would be more difficult. But, honestly, the more we thought about it, the more unsure we felt about adoption being the right route for us, anyway.

As we were looking for other options, Katie came across a relatively new procedure, Pre-genetic Diagnosis In Vitro Fertilization, or PGDIVF, for short. With this procedure, they would do a normal In Vitro procedure of harvesting eggs from my wife for implantation, but they would test them first so that only those without the genetic issue that causes Fragile X were implanted.

This felt right to us; it felt like it was an answer to prayer, and we decided it was what we needed to do.

The only problem was that it cost over $25k and it was not covered by insurance. We would have to come up with all of the money ourselves. That's a lot of money for anyone, but it was an obscene amount of money for us at that time. I had just graduated from college and was starting my career with entry-level work.

But, unlike almost everything else about the situation, this was something where I could do something to control the outcome.

Finally, I felt empowered, and I threw myself into it.

This decision reminded me so much of the example my parents had shown me about self-sacrifice and doing whatever it takes for your family, when I was growing up.

I felt like I was fighting for all of my children—the ones who were already born, and the ones who were yet to come. This felt like an obstacle I could overcome. I had to do it.

So, we started saving everything we could. We sold the old cars we had and bought a salvage title van. I rode my bike to work (which wasn't that bad until winter came). We ate lots of pasta and inexpensive food, and rarely went out. We sold a bunch of our stuff on eBay and looked for every possible way to save. We were doing our part and sacrificing whatever it took. Saving up and preparing for this procedure took nearly two years.

Two years.

The sacrifice we were making was purposeful and it gave us the discipline we needed to stay on track. Our lifestyle was a daily reminder of the commitment we had made to our family, to this procedure, and to the strong faith we had that this procedure was the answer to our prayers.

As you'd expect, I was closely tracking the money we were saving and the rate at which we were saving it. We committed to a date for the procedure. We had to fly a specialist in from the East Coast, and so once we committed to a date, it was locked in. However, as the date got closer, it became obvious that we were going to be a few thousand dollars short of what we needed.

I was at a loss for what more we could do.

We had given everything we had to this and, in just a few months, the specialist would be flying in to perform the procedure. So, there I was, desperate, and trying to figure out an alternative.

It was during that time that I read about a local fundraiser that had been organized to raise funds for a special cause. They were asking sponsors to pre-commit to a certain dollar amount for every mile completed by the runners in the race.

It seemed so simple.

A light bulb went off in my head. I thought to myself: "Hey, I've got legs...I can run!" I knew I didn't have time to organize a race, nor would I even know how to do it, so instead I thought I could just find a local race myself and have people sponsor me for every mile that I ran.

The more I thought about it, the more convinced I became that this was the solution. I could see a way for us to raise the last bit of money we needed. Now, the only problem with this idea was that I had NEVER run any kind of race before. Not a 5k, not a 10k, not even just a 'k'. Nada.

I also had no idea what it took to prepare for or run in an organized race or what the experience would be like. On top of that, I was really out of shape and very overweight. I had been eating super cheap (a.k.a. crap) food for almost two years as we saved money and had neglected my physical health in a way I never had before. But, even with those facts staring me in the face, I decided that I needed to do this.

So, I started looking for a race that I could run in and, in my mind, the longest race was a marathon. More miles would mean more money from anyone who would consider sponsoring me. I looked online for a marathon that I could run before the payment due date, and for one that was within a reasonable driving distance from where we lived. And, very fortuitously, I found one that met both of those criteria in Rexburg, Idaho.

The race was two months away. In fact, it was just two weeks before the final payment was due for our procedure. It seemed to be perfect and exactly what I needed.

So, I signed up. I told my dad about my plan and, in his typical fashion, he immediately offered to do it with me to help raise more money (though, eventually we decided he would do the half marathon and not the full marathon). Like me, my dad had never run an organized race.

We were the stereotypical case of the blind leading the blind.

I created a flyer called, "Can Fat-Men Run Marathons?" and started handing it out at work and to anyone I knew. In the flyer I explained what I was trying to do and why, and then asked for at least $1 per mile sponsorship for myself and for my dad in this race.

I'll admit that it was hard for me to hand out those flyers. Every piece of paper felt like an admission that I was unable to support my family without help. But, my level of conviction was greater than my pride, so I handed those flyers out to as many people as I could.

I've been so blessed to have awesome people in my life and, as I handed out this flyer, the generosity of our friends and my co-workers was humbling. In a very short time, we had enough money pledged to put us over the top for the procedure. I couldn't believe it.

Now, there was only one thing left to do. I just had to run the race.

Again, I had no idea what it meant to train for a marathon. I read a few things, but in my mind they all seemed like overkill. I wasn't looking to win the race, just finish it. Every training program I looked at seemed to be geared to the more accomplished, competitive runner. In my inexperienced mind, even the beginner training programs required too much time and too much running if all I was trying to do was finish one race; not start a lifetime habit of running.

I decided to do my own training program to get ready. I decided that all I needed to do was lose some weight and get my lungs back into shape by running 2-3 times each week. I figured I was young, and not too far removed from my competitive sports days, so I would be able to ramp up quickly; at least to the point where I could finish the race.

Needless to say, my training ended up being very haphazard. I'd just leave my house and start running until I got tired, then turn around and run back home. The next time, I'd try to run a little bit farther than I did previously. Zero sophistication or understanding as to what I was really doing. I didn't have nice running shoes; I had my beat up cross-trainers, calf-length cotton socks, basketball shorts, and a t-shirt.

I was so clueless.

The two months went by quickly. So much had happened, but I was so excited to be so close to the date of our procedure. I was so excited that we were going to make it happen. I couldn't wait to meet those kids waiting to join our family.

All I had to do was finish this race.

# CAN FAT MEN RUN MARATHONS?!?

## FUNDRAISER FOR CARVER KIDS & FRAGILE X SYNDROME

*Yes, of course they can...especially if there is the right motivation!!
For a father and a grandfather in Utah, that motivation is their
children and grandchildren with a mental disability called Fragile X Syndrome.*

### WHAT IS FRAGILE X SYNDROME?

Fragile X Syndrome is the most common cause of genetically inherited mental impairment. The spectrum of mental impairment ranges from subtle learning disabilities and a normal IQ to severe mental retardation.

In addition to mental impairment, Fragile X Syndrome is characterized by symptoms which include physical and behavioral characteristics and speech and language delay.

### HOW COMMON IS FRAGILE X?

Because Fragile X Syndrome is a genetically inherited impairment, it can be passed on in a family by individuals with no sign of the condition. Fragile X Syndrome is often misdiagnosed or left undiagnosed completely. Despite the fact that Fragile X Syndrome is the most common form of genetically inherited mental impairment, most people are unaware of the syndrome.

- One in 260 women is a carrier
- One in 3600 males is affected
- One in 4000 to 6000 females is affected

More and more scientific research and attention is being dedicated to the study of Fragile X Syndrome each year. There is currently no cure for Fragile X Syndrome, but hope continues to grow that someday one will be found. Early diagnosis and intervention programs are vital in helping children with Fragile X Syndrome develop to their fullest potential and to help young parents understand more about what they can do for their kids. Sadly, programs that offer these services are often in desperate need of funding to continue to offer these valuable services to families.

*The flyer I used to raise the money we needed for the procedure. I'll forever be grateful to the wonderful people who supported us.*

# CHAPTER 5

## Principle 4: Be Patient With Your Imperfections

*"All things are literally better, lovelier, and more beloved for the imperfections which have been divinely appointed, that the law of human life may be Effort, and the law of human judgment, Mercy."*

*– Ruskin*

F ew things take people off track in pursuit of reaching a goal and owning their life more than making mistakes. This is especially true when they're doing something unfamiliar and the number of mistakes exceeds the number of successes.

Too often, people hold themselves to an impossible standard of perfection, rarely giving themselves the same amount of grace that they so frequently afford others. This is a very common form of self-sabotage that will undermine your success every time. Mistakes can become convenient off-ramps from goals. You can dress them up with frustration, anger, sadness, and other emotions to help you justify taking that off-ramp, or, you can let them strengthen your resolve and not let them stop you from going after your goals. Either way, it's up to you how you choose to respond.

It's important to remember that everyone falls short of reaching their targets from time to time, but the fall only defines you if you don't get back up. I'll often tell my kids that there is a difference between failing and failure. They sound so similar, but they aren't the same thing at all.

Failing gives you experience that helps you improve and refine the course you're pursuing. It gives you additional information that empowers you to make better decisions. And it makes you stronger so you can bear the weight of the success you're going after. In a very real sense, failing is an integral part of the process of succeeding. In fact, the bigger your failings are, the bigger successes you've qualified yourself for.

In comparison, failure is quitting. It's experiencing the inevitable setbacks and obstacles found in the pursuit of what you want and then choosing to let them be the excuse you use to stop moving forward. Failure is what happens when you fail and then decide to not get back up.

This principle makes logical sense; much like the principle of Controlling the Controllable. However, once again, this obstacle isn't logical in nature; it's emotional. This type of emotional obstacle is much harder to deal with because it feels unseen. It's often found in those silent battles that exist in your heart and mind, when the only person who is going to celebrate your decision to get back up, is you.

The simplest way I've found to handle emotional obstacles, like failing, is to first embrace and recognize the emotions you're feeling. If you're mad, be mad. If you're sad, be sad. If you're frustrated, feel that frustration. When you recognize and identify that feeling, you validate it, and then you can control it, as opposed to letting it control you. Identify what you learned from it, and then how you can react differently next time. Then, move on.

One more thought on this principle—beware of comparisons. Every time our inner voice delivers a self-criticism, it is a direct comparison to someone else, to someone else's expectations, or to our own feelings of inadequacy.

There is value in comparing when it's done with the intention of discovering opportunities for improvement. However, most people don't use comparison correctly. Instead of using it as a tool for self-improvement, they use it as a tool for self-flagellation and self-abuse. It becomes something that reinforces a person's internal narrative of self-doubt, inadequacy, and even self-loathing.

When it comes to 'external' comparisons (comparing yourself to others or to what others' expectations of you are), remember two things:

First, it is never a true apples-to-apples comparison. We are all unique, with individual experiences and talents—this makes comparisons to others both invalid and inaccurate.

Social media makes this form of comparison very difficult to avoid. Open up any platform and you're instantly drowning in what you perceive to be other people's reality. Don't let yourself get sucked into someone else's highlight reel.

Second, one of the biggest rewards that comes from owning your life is realizing your fullest potential. External comparisons can result in becoming satisfied with your progress based merely on someone else's definition of 'best.' Be honest with yourself by taking a look at your current reality, and then by doing whatever you can to take small, incremental steps forward.

As a parent, I try to teach my kids to understand that they need to love themselves and to feel that they are deserving of love, especially from themselves. And just like it's not appropriate to bully other people, it's not appropriate to bully yourself.

You've got to be patient with your imperfections.

This was where I found myself on race day. It was an early morning in Idaho and while I had never run any kind of a race before, there I was. I had no idea what was about to happen as I stood at the starting line and, honestly, had I known what was going to happen, I don't know if I would have proceeded.

But, as I was about to find out, it was a race that was going to change me forever.

# The Race

The day before the race, we packed up the kids and made the four-hour drive to Rexburg. We had scoured the internet for the cheapest hotel we could find, and as we pulled into the parking lot, we understood the reasoning behind the low nightly rate. The place appeared to be something between a sketchy hostel and a scene from a horror movie where no one escapes alive.

We all packed into one room and, after we got settled in a bit, we started making the dinner we had brought with us from home. Caleb and Caitlyn were out of their routine and, even with the warm glow of the twenty-year-old TV to distract them, they had a hard time calming down.

It was not going to be a restful evening.

So, when my alarm went off at 3:30am, I was not in a good place. I was very tired and a little more on edge than usual. Honestly, when I got the race information and found out how early we had to be at the parking lot to be taken to the starting line, I thought it was a joke.

"Doesn't the race start at 8 am? Why do we have to be at the pickup at 4 am?!" I had asked my wife as I read the information to her aloud.

I quickly shut off the alarm, hoping it wouldn't wake Caleb and Caitlyn. I grabbed the peanut butter sandwich and banana I had brought for my breakfast, and quietly left the room.

My dad was waiting for me by our van, as we had planned. He looked at me and said,

"Are you ready to go?"

"I'm ready to go back to bed," I replied.

He smiled and got in the van. We drove to the pick-up point in total silence. Neither one of us had ever done anything like this before, so we didn't know what to expect. Our emotions were a conflicting mix of fatigue and anxiousness.

As we pulled into the parking lot, we saw 2 school buses with people milling about them. We parked and headed to join the group. And, while the entire group of runners easily fit onto those 2 buses, it seemed like a large group to me at the time.

As I scanned the group, I very quickly began to feel out of place. I heard them talking about their 'pacing' and 'splits' and other terms and phrases that were totally foreign to me. My old cross trainer shoes, cut-off cotton shirt, long-white cotton socks, basketball shorts, and golf visor stood in stark contrast to their dry-fit clothes, neon running shoes, and hydration belts.

I knew that I hadn't trained as much as I should have, but, up until that moment, I felt I had done enough to be able to at least finish the race. However, at that moment, I realized that there probably existed a minimal level of marathon preparation; and that I had not reached it. My only consolation was a handful of runners who were a little heavier, like me, and who all seemed to be wearing knee braces and headbands. As I looked at them, I thought, "If they can do this, I can do this."

The race organizers must have believed that it would enhance our experience if they had us there at 4 am, only to make us hang around for an hour in the freezing cold of an early fall Idaho morning. I couldn't help but think that I easily could have spent another 45 minutes in bed, asleep.

As we stood there trying to keep warm, I finally shared some of my anxiety at seeing the other runners, with my Dad.

"It'll be ok, Cim," he said.

He was calm and encouraging. It was easy for me to forget that this was his first race as well. I think that perhaps, when you've already sacrificed so much for your kids, you get comfortable with stressful situations, and uncertainty is more quickly evolved into greater conviction. His demeanor helped me to calm down a little.

Finally, we got on the old school bus and found a seat near the back. I couldn't bring myself to look anywhere, except out the window I was sitting beside, and every anxious exhalation fogged the window just a little bit more. The bus pulled out and began the trek to the starting line. It didn't take long before we were outside the lights of the city and into the darkness of the countryside. The only thing I could really see were the yellow stripes of the lane divider being illuminated by the lights on the side of the bus. I watched them fly by and, for the first time, I truly understood just how far it was that I was going to have to run.

My anxiety started to spike again.

As we got to the starting line, we were treated to almost another hour of standing around and waiting. At least they had some fires burning to ward off some of the biting cold.

Still, not much was said.

To me, it felt similar to that part of a roller coaster that slowly pulls you up to the highest point, and the closer you get to the initial drop, the more the nervous anticipation increases, until you finally crest the peak and plunge downward. Some people love that part of a roller coaster ride—I am not one of those people.

Finally, they had us head down to the starting line. I said, "Ok, pops, let's go do this." And then, in an attempt to encourage me, my dad accidentally gave me the worst possible advice you can give someone about to begin their first marathon.

"Ok, Cim, I know you're nervous…but I just want you to run. When that gun goes off, don't try and wait for me, just put your head down and start running. You can do this, don't be scared; just give it all you've got and go for it!"

Not having any other strategy in mind, my dad's last minute pep talk became my game plan. As I stood there at the line, I reminded myself that I was still in my 20's and that I had been an athlete my entire life. I thought about the money from generous sponsors and about my willpower to make this happen. I decided, with conviction, that God would bless me and that I would defy all odds and push myself to run the entire way—clearly, all common sense had escaped me.

Not good.

After the gun went off, I just started running like a madman. I was running fast…well, fast for me. About 200 yards from the start, I realized that I couldn't keep up with the main group of fast runners, but I was staying ahead of many others, and I started to feel like my 'strategy' to just run hard for the entire distance, could actually work. I even started reasoning that the quicker I ran, the quicker I'd be finished; so I pushed myself a little harder, visualizing the miles ticking by quickly like a car's odometer.

I've mentioned that I didn't have a clue what I was doing, right? Honestly, I was just some motivated fool out running the empty roads of Idaho that morning.

I don't remember exactly how long I kept up that ridiculous pace, but at some point, I realized I had better slow down, or I was going to die. Even I knew that you're not supposed to hit your physical limits within the first 5 miles of a marathon. So, I slowed down to a more manageable jog. And, after a few more miles, I adopted a walk-jog strategy.

Many of the people I had been ahead of, caught up and passed me. It didn't take long for me to fade towards the very back of the race. In fact, after about an hour of my walk-jog strategy, I realized that I was running all by myself. And, I'm not being metaphorical, I mean, I was really all alone. The bulk of the runners were now way ahead of me, and the handful of people with neoprene braces covering every visible joint they had, were still way behind me.

But, I didn't know any different, so I just kept going. The only thing that really let me know I was in the race, were the small mile markers on sticks, and the occasional water station along the course. Just before mile 12, the road I was running on took a gentle turn to the right and I followed it without giving it a second thought. As I was making the turn, I realized that it was actually a fork in the road, and that there was a hairpin turn that went to the left as well. I wondered if I was supposed to go that way...but in my overly fatigued mind, I reasoned that the gentle right turn I was following was the obvious choice.

So I kept going.

But, that left turn continued to nag at me. The first inkling I had that something wasn't right, was about 10 minutes or so later, when it occurred to me that I hadn't seen a mile marker for a while.

"That's kind of weird," I thought to myself.

"Maybe they don't mark every mile after a certain point," I innocently mused.

Dumb. Dumb. Dumb.

A few more minutes passed, and still I didn't see a sign. I was starting to get worried. I was literally in the middle of nowhere on an empty road.

A car came up behind me, surprising me even though it went wide on the road to give me plenty of room. Startled, I looked at the driver the car and saw that they were waving as they drove by.

"That's nice of them," I thought. "I appreciate the support," I said out loud.

Dumb. Dumb. Dumb.

I started focusing as far up the road as I could, to see if I could see an aid station on the horizon. But, there was nothing. It had now been about 20 minutes since I had taken that dumb turn. After another minute or so, I noticed the same car coming back in my direction. As they got closer, I noticed they were still waving.

"Wow, it looks like I've got some fans," I said to myself.

But, this time I looked closer, trying to see the faces of my marathon groupies. And I realized that they weren't waving—they were wagging their fingers at me.

"Huh?" I wondered. "Why are they doing that? Am I on the wrong side of the road or something?"

As the car approached, the window rolled down and the driver leaned out and said, "Hey! You're going the wrong way!!!" And then they continued to drive on by. They probably thought it would be breaking the rules to give me a ride back to the course.

Who the heck goes the wrong way in a marathon?! Apparently, I do.

"I'm such an idiot!" I yelled to myself.

All of a sudden, that overly quick start, my lack of preparation, my fear, and everything I had been battling that day, crashed into me like a ton of bricks.

I felt exhausted.
I felt defeated.
I felt stupid.
I felt out of shape.
I felt embarrassed.

I sat down, right on the asphalt in the middle of the road. I didn't care if I got hit by a car; I just wanted to be done. I started to cry tears of anger, frustration, and total fatigue. I couldn't believe it. I had gone the wrong way—as if a marathon wasn't long enough. The longer I sat there, the more I wallowed in those feelings. I just wanted to quit.

"What am I even doing here?" I asked no one, except myself.

Truthfully, I had known since the day I started collecting money, that everyone who agreed to sponsor me would give it to us no matter how I did in the race. Heck, these were good friends who probably would have given me the money if I'd just asked for it. Secretly, I had known all along that I was just running this race to feel like I had earned their money; that I hadn't asked for their charity, and that I had done my part to show them I was willing to do whatever it took and was worthy of their generosity.

But, at that moment, on that lonely road, that noble decision didn't matter to me. I knew I'd have a great excuse as to why I didn't finish—I'd gone the wrong way! We'd laugh about it and they'd pat me on the back and give me a hug and tell me I did my best and they were still happy to support me. We'd still have the money for the procedure and all would be well.

It took just a few moments to find every reason, rationalization, and excuse I'd need to justify walking away and no one would be able to fault me for it. Sitting on that warm blacktop, I had convinced myself of all of it. And, for a moment, those excuses made me feel happy. I was done with this race, I'd have what I wanted and everyone would be ok. Pain, over.

Then, I laid down on the asphalt and looked up at the blue sky. I just wanted to stretch for a moment. As I lay there, I thought about how I would reach Katie so she could come and get me, and thinking about her made me think about my two little babies who were with her at the race.

Caleb and Caitlyn.

They were somewhere out there, waiting for me. My family. In an instant, my mind went back to that fateful afternoon when I came home and found Katie crying on the couch. It had been nearly three years since that day, but not a day went by that I didn't revisit that moment in my mind.

I could still hear her voice as she told me that Caleb wasn't ok.

I remembered how lost I'd felt for so long and how dark I had let my life become. I remembered the pain and the frustration of being dealt that hand and how powerless I was to change it. I remembered feeling hopeless and afraid, unsure of what I had done wrong and why I was being 'punished.'

And then, I remembered the moment when things changed: "You are their dad, so act like it."

I remembered the clarity it gave me and how it had changed my perspective in an instant. I recalled how my mindset had instantaneously shifted and created a desire in me to do whatever I could to make things better. And, I remembered my two babies and the struggles they'd continue to face in their lives.

 If they could do that, then I could do this.

I thought about my beautiful wife and the courage that she had always shown in facing things, knowing that she blamed herself for the 'defective' gene no matter how hard I tried to convince her otherwise. I thought about how she never complained and how she never lost her faith.

 If she could do that, then I could do this.

In that moment, I understood for the first time that I wasn't running that race for the money. I was running that race because I was a dad, and dads do whatever it takes to take care of their families. And this? This was something that I could control. The purpose behind that race was bigger than the mistake I'd made. I couldn't change that I'd gone the wrong way, but I could choose how I was going to respond to  it. And, in a choice between quitting and carrying on, the choice was clear.

So, slowly, I picked my tired body up off of that empty Idaho road, and started running back. Every step back was hard because it felt like a wasted effort. It wasn't getting me any closer to the end of the race; I had to run it just to get back on course. About 20 minutes later, I finally arrived back to that fork in the road and, this time, I saw an arrow stapled to a stick and pounded into the ground leading in the correct direction.

I don't know how I missed it, but there it was. To say that my frustration reached another level would be a gross understatement. I was so mad at myself and I couldn't fathom, for the life of me, how I had missed the sign the first time. As I rounded the left turn, I noticed that all of the neoprene-knee-brace walkers were in front of me. I was determined not to finish last. Now, while I clearly didn't classify myself as a runner, I still had some youthful pride left in my veins, and I didn't want to lose to a group of glucosamine and chondroitin addicts who were just out for a stroll.

Just ahead of them, I saw that the course went up a series of three undulating hills. A hill, followed by a flat spot, then another hill, a flat spot, and then a final hill. I assumed that the walkers would go really slowly on those hills, so if I pushed myself, I delusionally reasoned, I could pass them.

As I arrived at the base of the first hill, I took my effort up a few notches and I passed the first two walkers. And, though I was pretty winded as I reached the top of it, I decided to go for it again on the second hill and pass the next group.

I started up the next hill, but about halfway up, disaster struck. Out of nowhere, a shooting pain began on the outside of my left knee. I attempted to 'run it off' for a few steps, thinking maybe it was a cramp or something, but to no avail. Every step delivered hot, shooting pain up and down the length of my leg. It felt like a stabbing knife. I limped up the hill, wondering what the heck had just happened.

As I neared the top of the third hill, I saw Katie. She was standing at the top waiting for me. As I got closer, the concern she had for me was written all over her face. I quickly explained what had happened—first about my knee, and then about going the wrong way, and asked her to take a look at my injury. Katie's degree was in sports medicine, but after a quick look, she said she didn't know what was wrong, but that she didn't think I should continue.

"I've got to finish this," I told her.

"Why? It doesn't matter, just get in the van. I don't want you to hurt yourself," she said.

I looked over and saw our van. Talk about temptation! It would have been so easy to just limp over and get in that van. I was hurt, Katie was telling me to, and my knee was definitely agreeing with her. But, my decision to finish had been made while laying on that warm asphalt a few miles back.

"I can't, babe. I've got to finish. I'm going," I told her.

To her credit, she didn't put up a fight after I told her that.

She just told me to be careful as I started limping away. I looked more like a speed walker than a runner at that point. And I still had 12 miles to go.

Consider my situation. On top of not being prepared and not having the right equipment, I had gone the wrong way, and now I was injured (I'd find out later that I had significantly injured my IT band tendon). It felt like everything that could work against me was working overtime.

But, one step at a time, I kept going.

Because of my limp, soon my hips started to really hurt, then my other ankle, and after a few more minutes, just about every part of my body was in pain. Apparently, my gait was throwing my entire body out of whack.

Each time I'd get to an aid station, I could see the concern on peoples' faces as I approached. They would ask me if I needed help, even offering to call an ambulance on several occasions. But, every time, my answer was simply, "I'm fine."

Truth was, I wasn't 'fine.' I was a mess. Every single step was a battle—physically, emotionally, and mentally.

And, as the race took me back into town, I came around a corner and saw a race volunteer who was taking down the string of flags along the race course. When he saw me, he tried to roll them out again and give me some words of encouragement as I made my way towards him. I also passed a nice, elderly woman who was watering a dead spot on her lawn with a hose. After looking at me, she just started spraying me down without saying a word. I didn't complain; in fact, I thanked her.

Slowly, the miles ticked by: 20… 21…. 22….. 23…… 24……. 25… finally 26. I never really thought that the .2 part of the marathon distance was a big deal. But, on that day, trust me, it was. I passed mile 26 and came around a corner. I remember trying to block everything else out except for the road in front of me.

Ignore the pain.
Ignore the exhaustion.
Focus on the road.
One step at a time, you're almost there.
You're not going to quit...this is for your kids...this is for your family.

Pain, so much pain.

As I rounded that final corner, I started down a picturesque street lined with trees. I could see the finish line and the banner that was strung across the road. It was empty, and I was alone. "How fitting," I thought. "I've been alone all day, why not now?" But, as that thought came out of my mouth, it was almost instantly met by a feeling in my heart.

"You haven't been alone. Not for one step."

It's obvious by now that I'm a person of faith, and one of the things I've found to be true is that, while we're asked to go through hard things sometimes, we're often given tender mercies to help us along our way. Little signs, indications, or feelings that are tailor made for us in whatever moment we find ourselves; when our hearts most need comfort. It doesn't mean that it makes it easy, and it certainly doesn't mean it removes the struggle, but sometimes we aren't supposed to know the why behind hard things.

And when we do our part, when the world feels too heavy for us to carry for one minute longer, and we continue to do our best with what we're given in that moment, He will never leave us feeling abandoned or alone.

"You haven't been alone. Not for one step."

As that thought entered my heart, I felt my mind and soul fill with peace. The pain was still there, but the mental battle had disappeared. I had fought the 'good fight,' and I hadn't given up. It was at that precise moment that I was given a tender mercy.

As I looked ahead at the finish line, I saw a little girl wearing a pink hat waving at me. It looked so surreal; it looked just like a picture. That little girl was my baby; it was Caitlyn. My little angel had left her lookout at the finish line to run out into the middle of the road and wave at me. Gratitude filled my heart and, with teary eyes, I ran (limped) to my little girl. As I finally crossed the finish line, someone put a 'finisher' medal around my neck and asked me if I needed a paramedic. "No, I'm fine," I said, for what seemed like the 100th time that day.

I don't think they believed me, but I didn't care. I limped over to where my family was. I hugged my dad, who was in tears as well, and thanked him for doing his part. I hugged Katie. Then, I fell onto the ground and I hugged my two kids;

I just wanted to hold them.

I had done it. It had about killed me, but I had finished the race.

*This is a picture of the marathon. I've run a few marathons since and never run as alone as I was that day.*

*All I wanted to do after I crossed the finish line was hug my wife and hold my kids. I got one of those things (the hug came after a shower).*

# CHAPTER 6

## Principle 5: Own Your Internal Narratives

*"We all have stories we tell ourselves. We tell ourselves we are too fat, or too ugly, or too old, or too foolish. We tell ourselves these stories because they allow us to excuse our actions, and they allow us to pass off the responsibility for things we have done—maybe to something within our control, but anything other than the decisions we have made...And it is past time, I think, for you to stop telling that particular story, and tell the story of yourself. Stop defining yourself in terms of them. You don't just have to exist in the empty spaces they leave. There are times in our lives when we have to realize our past is precisely what it is, and we cannot change it. But we can change the story we tell ourselves about it, and by doing that, we can change the future."*

*– Eleanor Brown*

**M**y dad once told me that there are life lessons all around me if I'd just stop and look for them. That advice has always stuck with me. As I look back over my life so far, I am amazed by how the life lessons I learned as a child, and then as a young adult, prepared me to handle the challenges with my precious kids.

Some lessons have been positive and uplifting, while others have been tough and challenging. But, these interconnected lessons have been woven together to form the fabric of my life. They have shaped how I see the world and they have impacted the decisions I make every day.

Your 'choices' are the decisions you make. This is really what 'owning your life' is all about; owning your choices. But here, I want to take it a step further once more.

Owning your choices means owning the outcome.

You must understand that the outcome is determined by what you do, or by what you don't do. Taking ownership of these foundational narratives will assist you by aligning who you want to be, and what you wish to achieve, with many other aspects of your life.

When we take ownership, we also accept responsibility for past mistakes, and for the necessary learning that comes along with them. Case in point—when I first found out that my kids had Fragile X, all I wanted was to be numb and escape. I didn't want to be present in that situation; I was hoping to just disconnect and then reappear once the tough time had passed. But it wasn't going to pass. I had to step into the trial—head-on, and with no assurances of how it would end up, but with the faith to know that I would figure it out.

And, as I began to be more conscious of the misalignment between the narratives I was telling myself and what I really wanted, I was in a position to be able to reframe them. As a result, I began to see the lessons that were presenting themselves to me, as well as the purpose behind them. It wasn't empty suffering, it was a refining and molding process that was designed to shape me into a better version of myself.

# Coming Full Circle

It took me a while to fully physically recover from that marathon. I felt a mixture of pride, relief, and embarrassment regarding my race day performance. For a long time, I didn't tell anyone, other than Katie and my dad, that I had run the wrong way on the course. It wasn't until many months later, that I finally got some perspective on what had truly happened to me that day on that empty road in Idaho.

I was still struggling to walk normally down the stairs in our condo, when we were thrown into the complexities of the IVF procedure we had sacrificed so much for. Anyone who has gone through this process will understand what I'm talking about.

Katie felt like a pincushion as she underwent a series of daily injections that put her egg production into overdrive. Then came the egg retrieval, followed by the genetic testing of the eggs for Fragile X. At the end of the cycle, we ended up with 3 fertilized eggs. The specialist told us that 3 was an ideal number, and that they recommended we implant all 3.

We agreed to that plan.

At first, I was nervous. I had quietly hoped to have more than 3, so we could freeze some to use later—should we decide to have more kids down the road, or to have 'extra' so we could try implantation again if, for some reason, it didn't work the first time. One thing that they had been very clear about from the beginning was, this wasn't a 'try it until it works' deal. You got one shot at it. If it didn't work, you were welcome to try again, but you'd have to pay for it all over again. And, with the level of sacrifice it had taken us to get to this point, I felt we were only going to have one shot to make this work.

We had one shot at this.

Those 3 tiny embryos were then incubated for a few days in preparation for implantation. During this process, the specialist we had flown in from the east coast kept making very encouraging comments about how well the procedure was going. She shared how 'strong' the eggs were, and told us how 'good' the fertilized embryos were looking in the incubation.

They gave us an ultrasound picture showing the 3 fertilized embryos. We put that picture on our refrigerator, next to pictures of Caleb and Caitlyn. We talked to the kids about the embryos, telling them that these were their brothers or sisters. We knew the chance of having all 3 'stick' once they were implanted was low, and that there were no guarantees of a pregnancy at all, but at this point it was hard for us to even fathom an unsuccessful outcome.

We had given everything we had—emotionally, physically, and financially. We couldn't have sacrificed more.

I felt as if we had walked through the 'refiner's' fire and were going to be rewarded for our faith and perseverance. Experience after experience indicated that this was part of a divine plan for our family and, while we didn't know if it would be 1, 2, or 3 babies who joined us, we were confident we had done our part to get the outcome we were hoping for.

While I had learned to accept that my plan and God's plan for our family wasn't always aligned, things were finally going smoothly and the feedback we were hearing was positive, so it felt to both of us that the two plans were finally in sync.

About a week after the eggs were implanted, we went to have Katie's blood drawn so they could do a pregnancy test. And the next day found us, yet again, nervously waiting by the phone, for yet another call from a doctor.

So much emotion, sacrifice, and faith had led up to that day, to that moment.

I can still picture that afternoon in my mind. Katie was sitting on the porch in front of our condo. Caleb and Caitlyn were playing on the grass and I was nervously pacing up and down the sidewalk. The air was cool for a late summer day, and Caleb had a runny nose—which often happened as the seasons started to change. Katie and I didn't really say much to each other—we didn't need to. We both knew what the other was thinking.

The ringing of the cordless phone Katie was holding broke the silence. She looked down at the caller ID and then looked up at me and nodded.

It was the doctor's office.

"Hello," Katie said. Then, a quick pause. "Yes, this is she."

I held my breath as I watched Katie; my entire focus was on her, waiting on every word that came out of her mouth, analyzing every facial expression she made in hopes of seeing an indication that she was getting good news.

But there was none of that. No smile. No nod of the head. She remained quiet, looking down at her feet, as she listened to the voice on the other end of the phone.

"Ok, I understand. No, that's ok. Thank you for letting us know," and she hung up the phone.

She lifted her head, and before one word left her lips, I knew what the answer was. It hadn't worked. Katie couldn't speak. She just shook her head as tears ran down her face. As I stood there absorbing the news, I felt my emotions transition from shock and sadness, to anger and frustration.

"No way!" I yelled, scaring the kids who were completely oblivious to the emotional blow their parents had just sustained.

My mind raced—I didn't know what to do or what to think. I went and hugged Katie, because that felt like the right thing to do, but honestly, I was feeling a lot of anger. I held her for a minute and tried to say the right thing, but the anger, the frustration, and the hurt was raging inside of me and I finally let her go so I could vent. I started pacing up and down the sidewalk again, but this time, I wasn't quiet.

"I can't believe this is happening," I said, trying to keep some composure for my wife, but feeling it quickly slip away. "There is no way that He would do this to us. This isn't how it is supposed to go! You do your best, you give it your all, and then He is supposed to make up the difference! We did…everything we could…"

I don't know when the tears came, but as those words escaped my mouth, I realized I was crying. "It was not supposed to go this way…" I said quietly as I sat down on the curb.

Looking down at the ground, all of the hurt, frustration, and feelings of betrayal started to feel very familiar. The darkness that I had previously walked through many months ago, threatened to rear its ugly head and push me back into the familiar comfort of its misery. I was once again at a similar crossroad and I had a choice to make. I could be bitter and angry and no one would be able to fault me for that. I could walk away, claiming that a loving God would never cause such pain.

But, I didn't want to go there again.

I knew where that path went and it wasn't where I wanted to go. I had learned that faith is tried so it can be tempered like steel and made stronger. I had experienced the tender mercies of heaven that let me know I wasn't alone and that the faith required of me made me stronger. I had felt the love of my Heavenly Father in my heart, and while I didn't know why things weren't working out like we had hoped, I did have faith that, in the end, it would be what was best for us.

I didn't know what else to do, so I prayed.

A simple prayer from my heart; that He would soften my anger, that He would quiet my doubt, and that He would bring peace to my heart. Not because I felt I had earned it, but because I needed that blessing so I could support my family. I prayed for faith and for the ability to hold fast to the truths I knew: that He was real, that He loved us, and that He had a plan for our family. I asked that someday, if it were His will, that I would be allowed to understand the purpose of this trial, but made the commitment right then, that even if I wasn't given this understanding, I would not let it canker my soul.

Katie came and sat beside me and put her head on my shoulder. "We're going to be ok. We'll figure something out," I said. I think she was a little relieved that I wasn't angry or shutting down again.

We started watching Caleb and Caitlyn, still playing in the grass. It was quiet for a few more minutes, and then I said, "So, today we're going to mourn. We'll mourn and let ourselves feel the pain of things not working out like we hoped, and having to say goodbye to the future that might have been. We'll give ourselves today. Then, tomorrow, we'll call the adoption agency again and get that process started — we'll see where that takes us."

Looking back, it's always been interesting to me that we never, at any point, questioned whether or not we should have more children. It was just a deep understanding. I believe that was part of His guiding hand, unseen by us, helping us down the path He had prepared for us.

And so, as it has a tendency to do, life soon went back to normal.

Katie gradually came off the medication she had been

taking for the IVF, and our busy life with the kids resumed. The hurt of the experience didn't really go away, but a feeling of peace returned to our home.

My career in training and sales management had started to pick up steam and I had to go on a work trip that took me first to Ecuador, and then to Mexico, for almost a month. And, in a seriously messed up twist of fate, the day after I got home, I had to jump on another plane to Texas for another few days.

Only one night home in almost a month. But it would prove to be a very important night home.

My only consolation at the time was that I had a week long family vacation coming up in a few weeks. We'd be travelling to California to see Katie's family for Thanksgiving.

Fast forward to Thanksgiving Day.

I got up and went to play basketball with Katie's brothers so I could try to justify the copious amount of pie I'd be eating later that day. I'm not sure if I came even close to burning enough calories to cancel out even one piece of pie, but I do remember that my shirt was drenched and I was ready for a shower as we pulled back into the driveway.

Not wanting anyone to beat me to the bathroom, I quickly made my way down the hallway. Katie came out of the bedroom and met me as I reached the bathroom door.

"Could you bring me some clothes? I want to jump in the shower before anyone else." I said.

"First, I need to show you something," Katie replied.

She handed me something. I took it from her and it took me a second to realize what it was. A pregnancy test. I looked at it and saw the two lines.

She was pregnant.

Katie just looked at me and shrugged her shoulders. A few seconds passed, but it seemed much longer as the implication of what she was telling me settled into my heart and mind. All of a sudden, the uncertainty about how we were going to grow our family, vanished. Katie was having a baby.

I hugged her, and as she looked at me, we both knew what the other was thinking without saying a word. Everything was going to be ok. Regardless of the outcome, everything was going to be ok.

We waited a little while before telling anyone, both because we wanted to make sure the pregnancy was going to 'stick,' but also, and perhaps even more than that, because we didn't want to deal with people's inevitable questions about 'what if…"

We spoke with our pediatrician and were very candid about our feelings. Due to the nature of Fragile X, we knew that if it were a boy, the likelihood of the child being more seriously affected was higher than if it were a girl. The pediatrician recommended an amniocentesis if the ultrasound determined that it was a boy Katie was carrying. This way, if the test came back positive for Fragile X, we would have time to emotionally process it before the baby was born.

A few months later, we went to get an ultrasound to find out the sex of the baby. After applying a ridiculous amount of cold gel onto Katie's stomach, the tech went to work. Heartbeat, check. Arms, fingers, toes, check. Measurements all looked good.

Then, the moment we had been waiting for. Personally, I have no idea how those ultrasound techs can determine what they're looking at when they do those things, but after some searching, the tech said, "Oh, there we go. It looks like you're going to have a boy!"

A boy. A boy!

For about thirty seconds, I was nervous. I had played out this scenario again and again in my mind. A boy meant greater risk for significant disabilities if he had Fragile X. A girl, a lesser risk.

But, I had also decided that I was going to be excited either way. No matter how this baby came to us, I was going to love it and be the best dad I could be. So, almost as quickly as the nerves came, I consciously decided to focus on the blessing of the news and I started to feel excited. We were going to have another baby boy!

We set up an appointment for an amniocentesis for a later date. During those next few months, Katie and I would talk about what would happen if the baby had Fragile X, but we decided we were going to try and not focus on it until we knew for sure, one way or the other.

Life was busy. Work was keeping me going 1000 miles an hour and Caleb and Caitlyn kept Katie going twice that fast. Our daily routines kept us from thinking too much about what might be. But, before we knew it, the day of the amniocentesis arrived.

As Katie laid back on the table in the doctor's office, we locked eyes. A deep understanding of what this could mean for us was shared even though neither of us said a word. The doctor slowly slid an obscenely long needle into her belly and I held my breath, fearing that he might hit the baby. And then, just like that, it was done. The doctor let us know that the amniotic fluid was going to be sent to a lab for testing and they'd let us know the results as soon as they were in.

"Great…more waiting," I thought to myself.

I don't know why I had expected them to do it during the same visit, but I was disappointed when they said it'd be a few days. Understanding our situation and sensing our anxiety to know the results, he told us he could call his office tomorrow to find out a more exact date. The next day, Katie called the office and they told her that the doctor would have the results in 2 days.

The day arrived and we did our best to be hopeful, while still guarding our hearts against news we prayed we wouldn't hear again. I stayed home from work that day to ensure I'd be there when the phone call came. We were anxious, without a doubt, but we did our best to stay occupied with the kids and to trust our faith.

The phone didn't ring that morning. More hours went by without a call.

Dang doctors.

I had decided to keep a long overdue dentist's appointment that was just down the road. I told Katie I'd be back in less than an hour and that I hopefully wouldn't miss the call. Of course, as things would have it, I hadn't been gone more than 5 minutes when my phone rang. It was Katie. I picked it up before it had finished the first ring.

"Did he call?" I hurriedly asked.

All I could hear were sniffles on the phone. Katie was crying and couldn't get any words out.

"Oh no," I thought to myself. "Not again."

I was just about ready to start consoling Katie, when she finally caught enough of her breath to let out the news I'd been waiting years to hear.

"HE'S OK!!! Cim, He's ok! The doctor said he doesn't have Fragile X!!" she cried.

"What?!" I yelled. "Are you sure? I mean, how sure was the doctor? What did he say?!"

"He said he was fine and that all the tests for Fragile X were negative," she said.

I couldn't drive. I pulled over to the side of the road and

cried with my wife. We celebrated the news we had hoped and prayed and sacrificed for.

It's impossible for me to convey in words what that moment was like. I have never felt a stronger sense of His love than I did in that moment. I ended the call and just sat there crying on the side of the road. I poured my heart out in prayer, not only expressing gratitude for the blessing we had just received, but also re-committing myself to Him to be a good steward of the things I had been blessed with—my wife and my kids. The familiar voice that had prepared and comforted me at the beginning of all of this, returned back to my heart and simply confirmed to me that there is a plan and a purpose for everyone, including me and my family.

I let the feelings of joy, peace, and love saturate my soul. And, once again, I felt my world start to pivot. But this time it didn't scare me because it was away from fear and towards a place of peace.

And then, just like that, the day came when our miracle baby would be born. Just like his big brother, Joshua decided to come into the world facing the wrong way (posterior). Labor was difficult for Katie, but we were so excited to meet our son. When he finally made his debut into the world, I instantly loved him every bit as much as I loved his brother and sister. I had wondered if it would be different, but it wasn't.

It was exactly the same.

He was so special, just like Caleb and Caitlyn were special, and I wondered what his role, his path, his life would be—

just like I had with the two that came before him.

When I held him, I thought about everything we had gone through to bring him to our family. I remembered how much we had changed and grown and how he had already made us better just by joining us. I found myself making the same commitments to him that I had made to Caleb and Caitlyn:

That I would do my best to be the best dad I could be. That I would be there for him no matter what. That he would never wonder if he was loved. That I would push him to be his best and to realize his potential. That I would always give him a safe place to push from as he learned to make his own choices and discovered how to own his life.

As we left the hospital, we covered his head in an, 'I love New York' beanie because I had just taken on a new work assignment that would be taking us across the country in three weeks. Probably not the best thing to do to your wife just after having a baby, but we felt it was the right move for us. So, we left everything and everyone we knew, and headed east.

The move was more challenging than I anticipated. Ensuring that Caleb and Caitlyn's needs were met within the school system added an extra layer of complexity. But, we figured it out.

And slowly, we settled into the routine of a normal life in our new home.

About a year later, Katie and I began talking about having more children. We were praying about it and letting the impressions of heaven settle on our hearts to help us know what the next step would be. Again, we began to have the undeniable feeling that our family wasn't yet complete.

However, this time, there wasn't no anxiety surrounding this decision. We were finally at peace with walking in faith in this area of our life.

We hadn't come to a final decision about how or when to bring our next child into our family when, unexpectedly, we were surprised with another positive pregnancy test. As we had learned with Joshua, when He says it's time, it's time— no matter what your plans may be.

We found out that we were having a little girl and we decided to name her Elizabeth, and call her Ellie for short. This time, we didn't do an amniocentesis, both because she was a girl and would be less affected if she had Fragile X, and also because we had moved beyond needing that assurance beforehand.

Come what may, the child would be loved in our home.

As Katie's due-date drew closer, Ellie still hadn't turned and was sitting breach inside of Katie, just like her sister. Katie and I still laugh about this—both of our boys came into the world upside down, and both of our girls came backwards. To be safe, the doctors scheduled a C-section to deliver Ellie.

Ellie's delivery was unique for us. We got up that morning, and Katie actually drove herself to the hospital while I got Caleb and Caitlyn ready and on the bus for school, and got Joshua to a babysitter. I was on my way to the hospital when Katie called to say they were waiting for me to take her in to deliver Ellie—it was almost like a baby delivery service.

This time, the C-section went smoothly and Ellie was born without incident. As we had discussed with the doctor beforehand, they took a blood sample they'd need to test for Fragile X during the delivery, so we wouldn't need to come in later to do it. And, while I was very aware of the test and what it could mean, it didn't dominate my thoughts like it had before.

As I met Ellie for the first time, I had this undeniable sense of peace that everything was right; that everything was just how it was supposed to be.

For the first time, it felt like our family was complete.

I didn't know if she had Fragile X, but I knew that she was supposed to be in our family and I loved her for making her way to us. I remember sitting quietly in Katie's recovery room the next day, holding Ellie while Katie slept and being overcome with gratitude for this little miracle. I softly cried as I promised my little girl that she would always be able to count on me, no matter what. Just as I had with our other children, I committed myself fully to doing whatever I could do to help her realize whatever Heavenly Father had planned for her.

Around a week later, we decided to take a day trip to Coney Island. It was one of those early spring days that's full of sun, but still just cold enough to make you anxious for summer to arrive. We went on a few rides and walked around the boardwalk for a while. Soon, the cold forced us back to our reliable, salvage-title minivan. Everyone's spirits were lifted from the fresh air and the family outing.

It was on the way home from Coney Island when Katie's phone rang. I looked in the rearview mirror, past Caleb and Caitlyn who were in their car seats in the middle row, and back to the rear seats where Katie was sitting between Joshua and Ellie's car seats.

Katie looked at her phone and said, "Cim, it's the doctor."

We had been expecting news on Ellie's Fragile X test at any time, but in the past, the doctors had always given us a heads up before calling with the results. So, I initially thought they might be calling to schedule a follow-up appointment or something with Katie.

I watched Katie through the rearview mirror as she answered the phone.

"Hello? Yes, this is Katie. Oh...ok," Katie said, and then she mouthed the words to me, "It's about Ellie."

Instantly, everything in my world paused and I was laser focused on Katie through that rearview mirror. To this day, I am convinced that guardian angels were flanking my minivan for the next 2 minutes because I was paying absolutely no attention at all to the road in front of me. I was hanging on every word she said, every gesture she made.

As Katie spoke with the doctor, I was desperately trying to find an answer in her tone of voice and in her facial expression. As soon as she hung up the phone, Katie looked at me through the rearview mirror, gave me two thumbs up, and a huge smile appeared on her face.

"She's ok! The tests were negative!"

We looked at each other, both understandably emotional. I said a quiet prayer of gratitude in my heart, and thankfully realized that I needed to pay attention to the road.

Ellie, another miracle baby, had found her way home to us.

I consider all of my children to be miracles of God's love.

The miracle of Caleb was how he helped me to understand what being a dad really meant, and to learn the real lessons of sacrifice that I'd need along the way.

The miracle of Caitlyn was the return of light and peace that she brought with her, just when we needed it most.

The miracle of Joshua was the re-committal of our faith—of having it tested and pushed to the limits—but ultimately learning that our path, although not always easy, is exactly right for us.

The miracle of Ellie was a key part of Heavenly Father's plan for us and our family. She was the culmination of this part of the narrative that He had prepared for us, and she showed us that even when we felt like we were walking alone, we weren't.

Around the time of Ellie's first birthday, we revisited the idea of continuing to grow our family. We talked about it, we prayed about it, but we both arrived at the same conclusion—

our beautiful family was complete. This was a bittersweet realization for us, but it was also very peaceful. We had fulfilled that part of our lives, and we were extremely grateful.

If you would have taken a picture of my family as I know it today and showed it to me back when Katie and I were just starting out, I would have seen perfection, just as I do now. It's exactly as I had imagined it to be. What is also remarkable is the wonderful, challenging, and refining growth that has happened to me since then. Looking back, I'm glad I didn't know what that process of growth would look like, because it would have overwhelmed me. But, I'm forever grateful for what that process did for me:

It made me stronger. It made me better. It helped me to truly understand what commitment feels like. It was more than being committed to the things that would make the highlight reel. It was being committed to the hard things as well. To the unexpected things. To the faith-challenging things. It was being committed to everything.

Because that's what dads do.

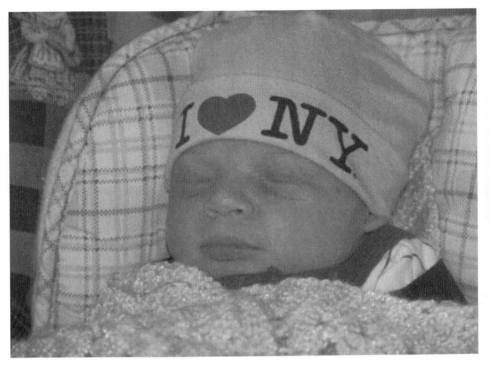

*Joshua the day we took him home from the hospital.*

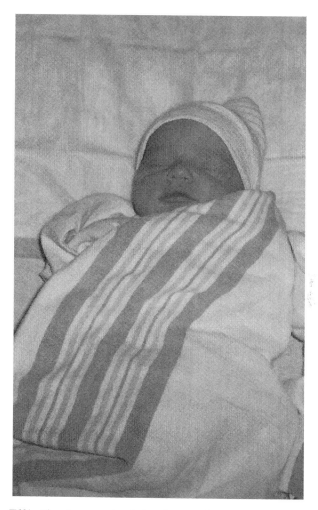

*Ellie the day we took her home from the hospital.*

*This is us. My family, circa 2016.*

# EPILOGUE

## The Crap Sandwiches and Ribeye Steaks of Life

*"And the day came when the risk to remain tight in a bud was more painful than the risk it took to blossom."*

*- Anais Nin*

The years between Caleb's diagnosis and Ellie's birth taught me a lot:

I learned that there is both purpose and progress in pain if we just look for it and aren't afraid to own it.

I learned that life sometimes contains unintentional wrong turns, but that those wrong turns don't have to define you.

I learned that purposeful effort is more valuable than any

innate skill or talent.

I learned what it means to be strong and also what true commitment feels like.

I learned that even when you do everything you're supposed to do, sometimes the lesson you're meant to learn is that you don't always get what you want (or, when you want it).

I learned that sometimes life gives you a big rib-eye steak, and sometimes it gives you a crap sandwich with extra mayo. And, while it's natural to want the rib-eye, occasionally a crap sandwich drops on your plate, and that's ok.

But, as you read this book, I hope you'll look at those crap sandwiches differently. I hope you appreciate them for what they are, and even though they're not enjoyable, they're the very thing that helps you to grow as a person. In fact, there really is no growth in the big rib-eye steak. There's enjoyment and comfort, but no growth. Growth is found in the lessons that come with the crap sandwiches, especially the ones with extra mayo. So, when they land on your plate, take the opportunity to learn from them.

Don't run from them, try to ignore them, or waste energy placing blame on something or on someone else.

Part of owning your life is owning the experiences found in the crap sandwich moments, because it's in these moments that you'll define, and also find, yourself. One day, you'll look back on your life and realize that those seemingly awful moments were when some of your most meaningful experiences occurred.⌐

Over the years I have seen, time and again, people who've grown comfortable running from life's challenges. Typically, when I work with these people, they tell me that they feel 'stuck' in their lives and that they aren't sure what they can do to change it. This consistent running away from challenges can lead to a long list of other detrimental behaviors: a struggle to maintain healthy relationships, a tendency to blame others, and a victim mentality. In addition, this type of reaction very easily becomes habitual, with the cycle of 'blame and run' quickly developing into a strange pattern of behavior that feels both natural and comforting. Yes, I said that. Feeling miserable can feel comforting. And if this habit continues, they will be on a road to mediocrity—not living up to their potential and expending way too much energy on defensively negative thoughts and actions.

Now, on the flip side, show me someone who deals with life's crap sandwiches with as much bravery and strength as they can muster, and I'll show you someone who is owning their life and becoming stronger. Show me someone who takes the crap sandwiches of life and pushes through them, and I'll show you someone who is inspiring and lifting other people up.

I can talk this talk because I walked this walk. In the beginning, I ran from the crap sandwich that was dealt to me and my family. I wouldn't own it, and all that did was make the situation worse. It also made me depressed. It wasn't until I stopped running that I found myself again. For me, owning that reality meant owning that I couldn't change the diagnosis, but that there were things within my control. I could control how I showed up for my kids, and I could control my perspective. I chose to run that marathon, and I chose to finish it. I chose to be the best husband and the best dad that I could be. I chose to own the situation and not let the circumstances define me.

Now, I am not saying that once I made that choice that everything was easy. Not at all. That will and determination of mine was tested—over and over again in the months and years that followed. To be honest, it is still tested from time to time today. However, I know, beyond a shadow of a doubt, that my power lies in my ability to choose how I respond to these challenges. I happen to life; life doesn't happen to me.

So, what about you? My dad once told me that life prepares you to handle any challenge that comes your way, if only you'll be aware of them.

Maybe you're feeling stuck.

Maybe you're so focused on the obstacle that you're blind to the solution.

Maybe you're reading this because a big crap sandwich has fallen into your lap and someone thought this story might help you.

Regardless, I want you to know that there is a reason, a purpose for whatever it is that you're facing. Choose to see the lesson and you'll start choosing to see the solutions. And, as you do this, you'll be better—even if it means you've got to eat a crap sandwich from time to time. If you need to make some changes, make them. If you're feeling tired, keep going.

If you screw-up, get back up and fight on. The process of becoming the very best version of you is worth every sacrifice and every inconvenience. Trust me.

Yes, it can feel risky to live up to these challenges and to truly own your life, and I'd be lying if I said there was no risk. However, there is risk associated with every potential path ahead of you. My advice? Choose the risk that points you in the direction of your ultimate goal.

I love this quote by Anais Nin: "And the day came when the risk to remain tight in the bud was greater than the risk it took to blossom."

You've got to learn to run your own race. It's your life, it's your race. You're the only one who can run it and, at the end, you're the only one who will finish it. It's your race—YOUR race.

Whatever sacrifice, struggle, or discipline is needed, it all just works to make you better.

You're worth it!

# THANK YOU FOR READING!

If you enjoyed this book and it had any impact on you that you'd like to share, I'd love to hear from you.

## StrengthOfHeartBook@gmail.com

# ABOUT THE AUTHOR

Cim Carver is a family man first. Professionally, he has served as an executive for many years in various capacities relating to sales, marketing, and training. He is a sought-after public speaker and leadership Coach.

Made in the USA
Middletown, DE
29 September 2019